Peter Gammer
2000

The Top End of Down Under

Photography by Peter Jarver
Text by Peter Jarver
and Kerry Davies

Thunderhead Publishing
Cairns

This book is dedicated to my wife Deborah, for her patience, understanding and help over the years. Also to John Keegan and Ken Duncan for their encouragement and inspiration.

First Published by Thunderhead Publishing 1986
1st Reprint 1986
2nd Reprint 1987
3rd Reprint 1988
4th Reprint 1989
5th Reprint 1991
6th Reprint 1993
7th Reprint 1994
8th Reprint 1997
9th Reprint 1999

Wildscape Australia
PO Box 549, Kuranda, Qld 4872 Australia
Ph (07) 4093 7171 Fax (07) 4093 8897
Email: jarver@thunder.com.au
Web: www.thunder.com.au

Design and Production by Grayt Art Studios, Sydney, Australia
Printed in Hong Kong by South China Printing Company Ltd.

© Peter Jarver and Kerry Davies 1986

Jarver, Peter, 1953-
The Top End of Down Under.

Bibliography.
ISBN 0 9589067 O X
1. Northern Territory - Description and travel - 1976 - Views. I. Davies, Kerry. II Title
994.2906'3'0222

PREFACE

Kakadu National Park was placed on the World Heritage List on 26th October 1981. It is one of the most important national parks in Australia. Its cultural significance dates back tens of thousands of years while its geological significance was born out of earth movements more than a thousand million years ago. The area is outstanding for its richness in flora and fauna, with extensive wetland areas providing the basis for its diversity. The scenic grandeur of Kadadu is characterized by vast floodplain areas lying at the base of an enormous escarpment which extends for some 500 kilometres. The often sheer-walled cliffs harbour numerous nooks and crannies which contain lush rainforest pockets, clear water pools and, at widely spaced nick points, thundering waterfalls. The magnificent spectacle of a flooded stream plunging 200 metres over a sheer drop is not easily forgotten. Most of Kadadu National Park is in a truly wild state and its preservation as such is extremely important, given the rapid pace of development in the Top End.

Darwin, the capital of the Northern Territory and the Top End, is a city of extreme multiculturalism and hectic construction activity. From being virtually destroyed by Cyclone Tracy in 1974, the city has rebounded dramatically into a vibrant, cosmopolitan place now characterized by high rise buildings, international hotels and an extensive arterial road network. The frontier town of only fifteen years ago, has been completely transformed. Its future is cemented in the fact that it is the largest town for nearly 2,000 kilometres and prominently placed to become Australia's gateway to the vast Asian area only 500 kilometres to the north.

Dominating both Darwin and the whole Top End is its unusual and intense climate. Extensive thunderstorm activity during a six month period, provides the water necessary for shaping its landscape and sustaining its population. With some 90 thunderdays a year, Darwin is the most lightning prone place in Australia. Enormous billowing thunderstorms roll through the Top End with great regularity, producing intense rainfall and providing incredibly spectacular lightning displays. Reaching to the very limits of Earth's weather producing atmosphere, these cloud mountains of the Top End possess shape and form unrivalled anywhere. The photographs here, collected over an eight year period reflect the beauty and extraordinary diversity which comes from something which we all take for granted – clouds. So the Top End of Down Under is a place of not only spectacular landscapes but also of beautiful skyscapes.

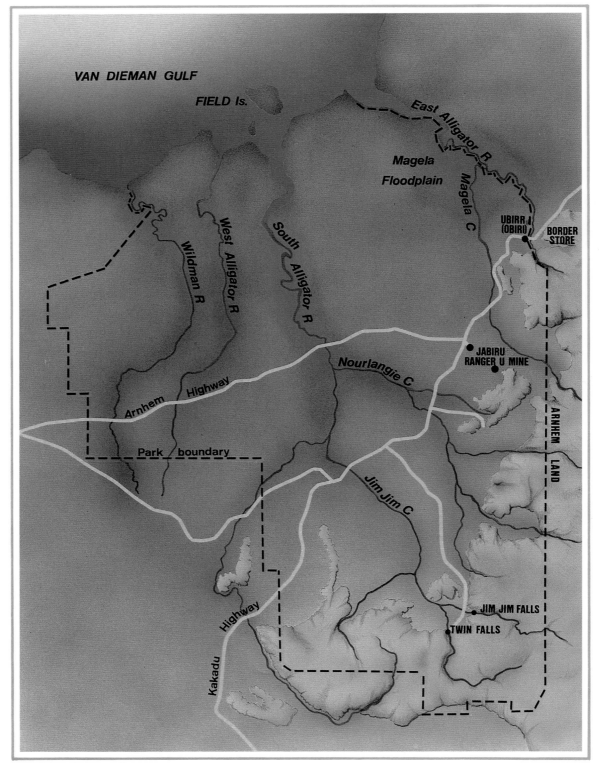

Kakadu National Park

Scale : 10mm - 9km

KaKadu National Park

1

National parks are usually places of outstanding natural beauty and sometimes of historical, scientific or cultural significance. The park may contain some outstanding geological formations or habitats of flora or fauna which are significant for their abundance or their rarity. The ecological communities present may be representative of a wider region or the area may quite simply, have intrinsic value for its scenic grandeur.

Kakadu National Park has all of the above. Its attributes make it one of the more outstanding national parks in Australia, and for this reason its inclusion on the World Heritage List was not only important, but inevitable.

The park is extremely rich in flora and fauna and, even though its area is only four per cent of the Top End, thirty-eight per cent of the total plant species may be found here. Its wetland ecology is unique in both its diversity and extent. Aquatic plant and animal life is prolific, which in turn supports vast numbers of birds. In fact, one third of all the bird species found in Australia are present in Kakadu. Herons, Magpie Geese, Whistling Ducks, Burdekin Ducks, Pygmy Geese, egrets, kites, White-breasted Sea Eagles, jabirus and brolgas are just some of the species to be found in abundance throughout the wetlands of Kakadu.

The extensive wetland areas flood each year when the monsoon rains arrive from Asia. The vast quantities of water which flow down the major creeks and rivers flush out and fill up the floodplain billabongs. By the end of the dry season, when water in many outlying areas has dried up, the floodplains become an important source of food for the abundant birdlife. With twenty-two frog and forty-five fish species present, the floodplains support a large and intricate ecosystem. Complementing all these animals are freshwater molluscs and crustaceans and many different types of aquatic plants, including the beautiful pink lotus lily. And among all of this teeming life roams the King of Kakadu – the saltwater

Jim Jim Falls in the early wet season

crocodile. At one time severely threatened by overhunting, the tide is now beginning to turn. Protected by legislation since 1971, their numbers have increased steadily over the last few years. The saltwater, or estuarine crocodile has habitats throughout the floodplains, billabongs and rivers, but further up the creeks toward the escarpment is the domain of the freshwater, or Johnston's crocodile, protected since 1964. The freshwater crocodile is nowhere near as dangerous as the larger and more aggressive saltwater crocodile.

The Magela floodplain and Yellow Waters are the two largest wetland areas, with the Magela floodplain covering an area of some 200 square kilometres in most years. One year in ten it will swell to 300 square kilometres – a veritable inland sea. The vast floodplains are fringed with dense stands of melaleuca. This beautiful tree is well adapted to the region's cycle of wet and dry seasons and only grows in areas which are flooded each year. Its common name, paperbark, is easily understood as the bark around the trunk is composed of numerous layers of paper-thin material. These paperbark forests are important habitats for numerous birds and animals and offer erosion protection during the heavy monsoonal rains.

Around one quarter of Australia's freshwater fish species can be found in the Kakadu region. This abundance is staggering. While the most extensive river system in Australia, the Murray-Darling System, contains twenty seven native fish species, the Magela and Nourlangie creeks alone contain twenty eight native fish species. This includes the well-known barramundi, the most sought after fish in Australia's tropical north. Although a good eating fish if caught in the sea, the many river and billabong barramundi in Kakadu may have a distinctly muddy taste, expecially later in the dry season. But the barramundi is not only of interest to the angler. Indeed, it is a most peculiar fish, undergoing a sex inversion during its life. Juveniles mature at three or four years

Lightning at midnight during a torrential downpour at the entrance to Jim Jim gorge. The entire scene here is illuminated by the lightning

of age as males, but change to females at the fifth or later year. Many of the really large barramundi of the billabongs and waterways have been fished out, but in years gone by some rather monstrous individuals, weighing up to twenty five kilograms, have been caught. Some of these hardy, wily individuals were reputed to have memories and appeared frequently in their own hunting areas.

But where does all the water necessary for such extensive and rich wetlands come from? Several major creeks, namely the Nourlangie, Baroalba, Jim Jim, Barramundi, Deaf Adder, Cooper and Magela creeks feed the vast floodplains, which in turn drain into the major rivers – The East Alligator, South Alligator, West Alligator and Wildman rivers.

Following the creeks and rivers upstream, the land is predominantly flat or slightly undulating, until it meets a formidable barrier – the escarpment. Towering above the surrounding countryside, the often sheer-walled sandstone escarpment winds its way for some 500 kilometres, rising from 100 metres in height at the northern end of the park to an imposing 200 metres at the southern end. Apart from vertical cliffs and stepped cliffs, long talus slopes stretch out on to the undulating lowlands, and massive boulders may be found up to one kilometre from the base of the escarpment. Weather-worn and eroded, fantastic shapes may be found along the escarpment face and associated outliers. Individual columns of rock may teeter on the balance point, natural arches span huge widths and damp, dark caves and rock overhangs are found along the entire length of this imposing rock wall.

But perhaps even more dramatic are the magnificent waterfalls, which occur at widely spaced nick points where the major creeks that run across the plateau plunge over the escarpment. From perhaps a mere trickle in the dry season, these watercourses swell into thundering waterfalls with the onset of the wet season. Huge volumes of water plunge over vertical precipices producing spray and mist that can rise back to the top of the escarpment.

Jim Jim Falls after a heavy overnight thunderstorm. Heavy mist
swirls around the 200 metre high escarpment

The most impressive of these waterfalls is Jim Jim Falls. With a sheer drop of 200 metres, the watercourse has carved out a huge gorge; the size is immense. The escarpment walls dominate the whole area, towering to a dizzying height, pronouncing the insignificance of the observer who has managed to walk to the deep, dark splashpool of this mighty waterfall. During the Wet the mist and spray are relentless, driven by gale-force winds produced by the power of the waterfall. Two smaller falls lunge out from the escarpment, one on each side of the main falls. To be alone with this magnificent spectacle can generate a feeling of primordial existence. Indeed, it can feel as though you are the first person to ever discover this hidden wonder.

Though not as overpowering as Jim Jim, Twin Falls is equally outstanding. This waterfall is situated several hundred metres up a snaking gorge. The steep, mostly sheer cliffs of the escarpment give way to lush pockets of rainforest lining the gorge and the splashpool is edged with a white sand beach. The name is derived from the fact that the single stream diverges into two separate waterfalls which cascade in several stages down the 200 metre escarpment. A diverse area, little nooks and crannies of the gorge hold many surprises, including additional small waterfalls, caves of varying sizes and smooth white sand beaches.

Many other smaller waterfalls may be found along the length of the escarpment. Most stop running altogether in the dry season, but a few are fed from springs and so continue trickling all year round, waiting to be filled again by the wet season torrents of rain.

Along the escarpment, pockets of rainforest reside in sheltered rocky sites. A large evergreen dominates these forests, which also contain many other non-eucalyptus trees and beautiful Carpentaria palms, with their long slender trunks and symmetrical delicate crowns. When fruiting, their bright red berries stand out vividly from the soothing green of the canopy.

Rainforest tree leaning out over Jim Jim Creek. Spray and mist drift down from the falls at the left, and the normally placid creek churns into white water

Behind the escarpment extends the Arnhem Land plateau. Rising to heights of up to 500 metres, this inhospitable land comprises ancient sedimentary rocks carved and shaped by faulting and jointing. Over 1500 million years old, this plateau is in retreat, pushed back by the forces of erosion over eons. The copious amounts of water which drain off its rocky surface form the creeks and rivers which give the Kakadu area its special character. The headwaters of all the major creeks and rivers are in this plateau area, with the South Alligator River having the largest catchment area, of some 12,000 square kilometres.

As the wet season thunderstorms deluge large areas with high-intensity but short-period rainfall, the creeks and rivers rise and fall in unison. Rainfall intensities of over 100 millimetres per hour are not uncommon. Placid creeks may very quickly turn into thundering torrents. The deep cracks and crevices of the broken stone surface of the plateau slow the draining of the rainwater and a single thunderstorm will ensure the creeks flow for several days. The duration of flow during a season varies markedly and is related to the beginning and end of the wet season. The Magela flows for anything from 80 to 180 days a year. All the streams flow in a general north-westerly direction across the plateau and down through the lowlands to discharge through the extensive floodplains. Interestingly, the channels of the Magela, Jim Jim, Barramundi and Nourlangie creeks do not continue to the major rivers. Instead, they divide and distribute their water over the wide floodplains, which may be inundated for three to nine months each year, depending on location and rainfall.

Apart from consistent thunderstorm activity, the other major influence on rainfall is the north-westerly monsoon. As this airstream converges into heat lows over northern Australia, reliable heavy rainfall is produced and showers may be evident for days at a time. Fine, hot spells intersperse the rainy weather, but the coolness of the air is a major benefit of the wetter days with their

*Water lilies and water grasses in a small billabong. The white
flowers are only about 1cm. across*

extensive cloud cover. A third and unpredictable climatic factor is the tropical cyclone. These mighty storms unleash intense heavy rainfall over restricted areas and, although wind damage as far inland as the Jabiru area is unlikely, flooding can cause major problems. A cyclonic disturbance can be expected to affect the area about once in every three years.

Kakadu has special significance for the Aboriginal people. Aborigines perceive the landscape in a very different way to Europeans. They consider their ancestral beings to have formed the topographic features as they travelled over the landscape, giving it shape and features where previously there had been none. Tracks based upon routes used by these Dreamtime beings traverse the area, often converging on a prominent topographic feature, which embodies their spiritual significance. At birth Aborigines acquire a personal Dreaming. This requires specific obligations and rights for that person in relation to the relevant tracks and prominent features. Aboriginal people are thus inseparably linked with their land through the Dreamtime.

The Lightning Dreaming is one of many such Dreamings in Kakadu. Namarrgun, the lightning man, runs wildly through the country during many months of the year. This figure is depicted in one of the galleries at Nourlangie Rock, with stone axes attached to knees, elbows and head. As Namarrgun runs, the axes strike trees or rocks, creating lightning bolts.

The rock art provides, to a certain extent, an historical record of the area and for this reason Kakadu has attracted much attention from archaeologists and anthropologists. This area was one of the first in Australia to be settled by the Aboriginal people, more than 30,000 years ago. Though it is not possible to date the paintings themselves, pieces of ochre from some sites have been dated at 25,000 years and there is also evidence of the world's oldest edge-ground axes.

Large paperbark trees and water lilies growing in a permanent
swamp

There are many documented Aboriginal sites throughout the Kakadu region, and these can be divided into places of occupation, sacred sites and art sites. The latter are concentrated along the escarpment and its outliers. Frequently, though, important art sites are also occupation sites. The deep rock overhangs that protect the artwork from the rain also provide excellent wet season shelters. Sacred sites, perhaps a waterhole, cave, hill, gorge or rock formation, are endowed with spiritual associations. These sites are often accompanied by paintings or stone arrangements and certain important sites may be subject to secrecy, prohibition or danger.

Contact with other cultures has been occuring for many hundreds of years and is evidenced in the rock art of the most recent period. Possibly the first meetings were with Macassan trepang fishermen from South-east Asia. The praus with their distinctive shape and oblique sails feature in many rock painting sites. European sailing ships of many types are also depicted, perhaps recording the intermittent presence of the earliest explorers from England, Holland and Portugal from the seventeenth century.
Regular European contact was not made until the nineteenth century when British occupation of their land introduced new subjects to the paintings – guns and steel axes. In the short time since this, the Aboriginal people have been catapulted into the best and worst of European society.

In 1978, the Kakadu Aboriginal Land Trust was given title to the area, including the excisions made for the uranium mines of Ranger, Jabiluka and Koongarra, which pay mining royalties to the trust.

The Kakadu people leased the area back to the Commonwealth government and on 5 April 1979, it was proclaimed as Kakadu National Park. A second stage outside the Aboriginal land was added several years later and the park now encompassses

*Pandanus palms, swamp mahogany trees and paperbark saplings
on the edge of the Magela floodplain*

an area of nearly 13,000 square kilometres. A third area, the headwaters of the South Alligator River system, is proposed to be included in the National Park, but has not yet been proclaimed.

In 1969, a pre-planning committee from the Northern Territory Administration which had been studying the area summarised their findings with the following:

We are convinced that within the area there are ingredients of scenic grandeur, interesting and unique fauna and flora, and cultural and historical elements, which if blended and managed successfully will produce a great park for public interest and enjoyment as well as making a major contribution to conservation needs. This park will be unique in Australia, it will rival in national importance great overseas parks, and it will be a priceless gift from the present to later generations.

As a national park, we are endowed to manage the Kakadu region for present and future generations. Let us manage this spectacular area in a truly responsible way.

Rainforest on the steep walls of Twin Falls gorge. The Carpentaria palm is native to the Top End

Large paperbarks inundated by the annual overflow of the Magela Creek

*Roots of a young banyan tree contort themselves over moss-covered
rocks in Twin Falls gorge*

Beautiful light reflects off a tiny creek, fed by crystal-clear spring water

Pandanus palms and sedge grass in a swampy lowland

A wave of bamboo showers the bank of the South Alligator River

Twin Falls in the early morning

Rainforest overlooks the splashpool of Twin Falls

A small waterfall cuts its own gorge adjoining Twin Falls gorge

The top cascade of Twin Falls overlooks the gorge

Sheer-sided walls of Twin Falls gorge

Typical broken sandstone outcrop near the East Alligator River

Dry season bushfires burn large areas almost every year

A spectacular wet season sunset on Jim Jim Falls. Two additional small falls flank the main fall

An early morning mist envelopes Yellow Waters

A long-disused mountain of empty cans

*Red-helmeted, green-footed spraypainter blends in well with the
newly constructed processing plant of the Ranger uranium mine*

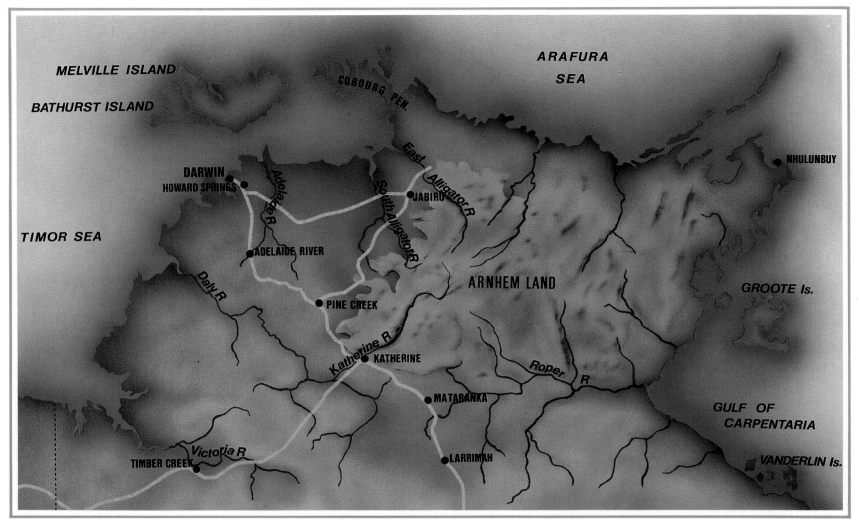

Top End of Northern Territory

Scale : 10mm = 45km

Darwin and the Top End

2

It was not the magnificence of the scenery that was in the minds of the British when they first sought to establish a settlement in the far north of Australia. During the saga of European rivalry in the East Indies, fears of French or even Dutch claim over the north of Australia and eagerness to establish a trading station to lure the wealth of South-east Asia prompted Britain to send Captain Gordon Bremer to lay claim to the land as part of the colony of New South Wales.

This he did on 20 September 1824 at Port Essington, though it took only a few days for the small party of soldiers and convicts to move on, due to lack of fresh water, to Melville Island where they established Fort Dundas. The settlement, however, and the later Fort Wellington at Raffles Bay on the Cobourg Peninsula were abandoned in 1829, despite the determined efforts of the settlers to endure the overbearing conditions of the tropical north. Indeed, the assessment by Matthew Flinders, on a navigational voyage in 1803, of the Territory's north-eastern coast was of a land "afflicted by fever and flies, fit only for a college of monks whose religious zeal might cope with suffocating heat and musketos which admitted no moment of repose".

A third attempt at settlement was made in 1838, again at Port Essington and again under the command of Captain Bremer, who named it Victoria for the British monarch. The following year the promising beginnings of the settlement were dashed by a great cyclone. Yet the people rebuilt the township. In 1843 the settlement was decimated by a severe form of malaria, probably introduced by the crew of one of the supply ships from Timor. The trade that had been hoped for did not eventuate the land was found to be unsuited to agriculture and the settlement languished. It was abandoned in 1849, the British finally conceding defeat.

It was not for another twenty years, and a further failed settlement, that the present site of Darwin was to be established. Overland exploration of the Northern Territory, notably by John McDouall Stuart in the 1860s, again stirred enthusiasm for northern

Lightning strikes the sea near Hotel Darwin, a building which
survived World War Two bombing and Cyclone Tracy

development. This time it came from South Australia in a bid for new pastures and the dream of a tropical paradise – and future land speculation and settlement.

In 1863 the government of South Australia won its quest for control of the Northern Territory and the following year the first Territory land sales were held simultaneously in London and Adelaide, for land which no one had seen and which had not been surveyed. It was sold in 160-acre agricultural blocks at a low 7s 6d per acre for the first 250,000 acres, with a free half-acre town lot thrown in. The revenue raised was to offset the cost of governing the new Territory.

South Australia's first attempt at settlement was led by Colonel Boyle Travers Finniss, who selected a site called Escape Cliffs at the mouth of the Adelaide River. It was a poor choice, however, surrounded by mangrove swamps and with most of the land flooding in the wet season. Finniss was on poor terms with his men and with the Aboriginal people of the area and he was ordered back to Adelaide in disgrace a year later, with still no survey work underway.

Finally, George Goyder, Surveyor-General of South Australia was appointed to select and survey a settlement site in 1869. From careful examination of earlier charts and journals, Goyder decided that Port Darwin was to be the site of the principal township of Palmerston. The large natural harbour had been discovered during exploration work by John Lort Stokes aboard the *Beagle* in 1839, and it was named after an old shipmate who had sailed with him in South America and was later to achieve notoriety for his theory of evolution.

Within seven months the work was complete, and the town of Palmerston, now the city of Darwin, bore the names of Smith, Maclachlan, Bennett, Knuckey, McMinn, Woods and Mitchell, all men of the survey team. And one of its earliest suburbs took the name of the Larakia (Larrakeyah) people, whose land it was.

Northern suburbs after Cyclone Tracy devastated Darwin in 1974

There is much in the story of the beginnings of settlement in the Northern Territory, of the aims of the first settlers and their governors, that is echoed in the character of present-day Darwin. Just as defence and trade were the main reasons put forward for the establishment of a northern settlement, today they both have a vital role in Darwin's existence, though circumstances, of course, have changed dramatically.

It is often said that the city of Darwin is maintained primarily for the purpose of defending Australia's vast and sparsely populated northern coastline. Historically Darwin's development owes much to the northern defence objective.

In 1938 Darwin attained a small regular army unit, the Darwin Mobile Force, based at the Larrakeyah Barracks, for the purpose of northern defence. By 1941, with Japan poised to enter World War Two, several battalions of the volunteer Australian Imperial Force were sent to Darwin in readiness for the outbreak of war in South-east Asia. When Japan attacked Pearl Harbour and Malaya in December that year, most of the Darwin-based troops were deployed to Singapore, Ambon and Timor, to be decimated by the Japanese forces.

It was believed that Darwin would soon be invaded, and by the end of February 1942 some 14,000 Australian and 3,000 American troops were stationed in the Top End. They were ready to defend against a land-based attack, however, and had little naval or air support. Darwin Harbour saw much activity in these months but most of it was for refuelling and for the transport of troops and supplies. Naval defence comprised one armed merchant cruiser and four anti-submarine corvettes. The airstrip at Batchelor, just to the south, had been expanded to a full air-base, mainly for American bombers active in the Philippines, and Darwin's R.A.A.F. base housed only three fighter squadrons, two of which had just returned from fierce fighting to the north.

Safety House, Mitchell Street, has its entrance ramp steam-cleaned

When the Japanese did attack Darwin, on 19 February 1942, it was from the air. At 9.30am a squadron of close to 200 Japanese aircraft was seen passing over the Bathurst Island mission towards Darwin. The R.A.A.F. base had, in fact, some twenty minutes' warning of the approaching planes. The mission was operating as a coastwatch, as were other coastal Aboriginal communities, but their warning apparently went unheeded.

The harbour and wharf area took the brunt of the attack, with twenty-two ships lost. The Esplanade area above the wharf and down to the Larrakeyah hospital was bombed and strafed with machine-gun fire. The R.A.A.F. base was also hit badly. At least 243 people were killed, thirty-seven of them civilians. The civilian toll would no doubt have been much higher had there not been a mass evacuation in previous months, reluctant though many people were to leave.

Air-raids became almost commonplace in the Top End over the next two years, sixty-four of them over Darwin. The whole of the Territory was placed under military control and troops teemed in. There were further evacuations of non-Aboriginal civilians and Aborigines along the coast were moved into camps, many of them to work for the army.

The task of servicing the vast population of troops raised industry to its highest level ever. The problems that had beset the pastoralists, farmers and others in the past – shortage of workers, high capital costs, transport and communication difficulties – suddenly disappeared. The war effort provided an almost limitless supply of labour and money; roads and airstrips were built, communication systems, power and water supply were greatly improved. When the war ended, in 1945, the Commonwealth government, which had controlled the Territory since 1911, was no longer so complacent about its northern development. The war had ensured a steady stream of funds and the push for development began in earnest.

An air-conditioner's water pipe stains a newly painted brick wall

Today Darwin still has its Larrakeyah Army Barracks, overlooking the harbour, and the navy has its barracks, HMAS *Coonawarra*, inland, down the Stuart Highway. The R.A.A.F. retains an imposing position in the middle of the ever-expanding city, which has grown around the base and Darwin airport. As a result, the sound of commercial aircraft and Mirage fighters on routine manoeuvres is a part of life in Darwin.

The operations of the naval base these days are largely in coastal surveillance work. Drug-runners and foreign fishing vessels are generally the targets. In March 1985 a fleet of Indonesian boats was spotted off Melville Island and two of the vessels were towed into Darwin by HMAS *Ipswich,* where the skippers were charged with violating Australian territorial waters. They were from a small Indonesian island village, and explained that they operated without navigational equipment, on the basis that when the sea turned muddy they had crossed into Australian waters and that the sea had been blue when they were picked up. They were promptly sent on their way home by the court, their catch and fishing gear impounded as penalty.

During the mid to late 1970s the catch was of a different kind – the Vietnamese "boat people" were arriving in great numbers, alarming the government with their determination to reach Australian shores. They were soon given refugee status and many stayed in Darwin to join an already highly multicultural society.

In fact, Darwin is often described as being more a part of Asia than of Australia, as much a result of its Asian population as of its geographical situation and climate. Like the Vietnamese, Timorese refugees arrived in Darwin during the 1970s following the Indonesian invasion of East Timor, and some are still trickling in under an agreement between the Australian and Indonesian governments.

Stairwell of a modern Darwin building

53

But the Top End's links with Asia go even further back than the first European settlement, to the trepang fishers from Macassar on what is now the island of Sulawesi. By the time Matthew Flinders witnessed their presence there in 1803, the Macassans were operating a well-organised seasonal industry. They would come on the monsoon winds in December and January and make semi-permanent camps along the coast, collecting and preserving the trepang. When the south-easterly winds of the dry season made their homeward voyage possible, they left to sell their produce in the markets of Asia. Their relations with the Aboriginal people were varied, but their visits brought a valuable cultural exchange and some Aboriginal people travelled back to Macassar with the returning boats. The Macassans introduced the dugout canoe, iron tools and tamarind trees. But the trepang industry was stifled in the early 1900s, however, by the levy of customs duties and licence fees, and then an outright ban in 1906 put a stop to the Territory's first industry.

There was also a time in the Top End's history when the Chinese outnumbered Europeans by a massive four to one. During the construction of the overland telegraph line from Port Augusta to Darwin in the early 1870s (the Territory's first development project), gold was discovered near Pine Creek (giving another boost to the town of Palmerston). There was a rush of sorts but the gold was not easily recoverable and large companies soon took over the diggings. These companies sought cheap labour to work the fields and the government agreed to import Chinese labourers from Singapore.

The first group of 200 arrived in 1874 but open migration saw the population grow to around 7,000 by 1888. They worked the goldfields, they laboured on the construction of the Palmerston to

Spraypainter makes a close inspection of a partially painted wall

Pine Creek railway, they established market gardens which supplied the townships, they served in the houses of the Europeans and they established themselves in the fishing industry, trades and stores. The economy of Darwin was largely in the hands of the Chinese (as it was in many parts of South-east Asia).

Though European racism was not as vehement as it was in the south, the Chinese were generally shunned and were resented for their economic hold on Darwin. In 1888 a tax was placed on Chinese people entering the Territory. With many leaving the country and the introduction of the "White Australia" policy in 1901, further decline of the Chinese population was ensured, and by 1921 it stood at 355.

Darwin's Chinatown, in Cavenagh Street, was destroyed in World War Two, during the first air-raid and subsequent looting. It was never rebuilt. The N.T. Administration, under direction of the Federal government, saw the war as an opportunity to replan Darwin and took over all property, issuing two week tenancies to all-comers. By the time this ruling was lifted, several years later, the Chinese businesses had been established in other areas.

Today Darwin is home to fifth and even sixth-generation Australian-born Chinese and, while their community is strong in itself, their contribution to the community at large is valued highly. Indeed, the Chinese are more firmly embedded in Darwin's foundations than most of its European population.

Smaller communities of Japanese, Indonesians, Malays and Filipinos also have an early stake in Darwin's history. Most were involved in the pearling industry, which began in 1884. It was not a steady industry but contributed to the economy at various times right up to the early 1970s.

Flying toward Darwin over the South Alligator River

Darwin's connection with Asia extends beyond its multicultural background. Not dissimilar to its British predecessors, the current Northern Territory government considers trade and economic cooperation with the countries of South-east Asia, as well as the Western Pacific region, to be the key to the Territory's future economic development. Government and business links in the region have brought Asian investment in several Darwin development projects including its new Performing Arts Centre.

Joint ventures now exist with the Taiwanese in prawn trawling and a pilot prawn farm at Middle Arm in Darwin. Another joint venture in the fishing industry has begun with Thailand, despite some protest from the local industry that the northern fishery is already under strain.

Exports from the Territory to South-east Asian markets include live cattle, buffalo and horticultural produce. The government is establishing a trade development zone on the east arm of Darwin harbour, which it sees as "cementing the Territory's status as a secure investment area and business centre". The aim of the zone is to create new export-orientated manufacturing industries and attract investment from South-east Asia and the Western Pacific. The controversial Darwin-Alice Springs railway, which the government has announced will be built with private funds, is also seen as advancing this aim.

Promotion of the Territory as an Asian tourist destination is receiving attention as well. But for the present, at least, there are probably more Territorians spending their holidays in Asia than the other way around.

Darwin is home to some forty-five nationalities and ethnic groups: apart from those of Asian origin, there are sizable communities of Greeks, Germans and Italians, as well as people from other parts of Europe, the U.S.S.R., the Middle East, Africa and the Pacific. Greek migration began in the early 1900s but many

Sprucing up a cruise ship, the long hard way

came in the 1950s from the island of Kalymnos and in the '70s from Cyprus. Its multiculturalism has provided an interesting feature in education. Community language programmes, courses in the languages of neighbouring countries and international student and teacher exchanges give recognition to the high proportion of students from non-English speaking backgrounds – the highest in Australia.

For many of the Territory's Aboriginal people, some 25 per cent of the total population, English is not their first language. In the Top End there are twenty major languages. Kriol, a composite of English and various Aboriginal languages is the most widely spoken of these, as it is used both as a main language and as a second language between disparate groups. In some of the remote Aboriginal communities, where traditional culture prevails, the schools conduct bilingual programmes, in English and the local language. Kormilda College in Darwin provides a bridging programme for Aboriginal children from remote areas, from which they enter the mainstream education system or continue to a post-primary programme. The college also operates as a hostel for Aboriginal and non-Aboriginal children from remote areas. Batchelor College has begun to turn out graduates of its Aboriginal teacher training course, unique in Australia. Darwin's Institute of Technology has its Aboriginal Task Force, aimed at preparing Aboriginal students for employment or further study and addressing the present limitations in Aboriginal education.

Most of Darwin's Aboriginal population, like the bulk of Darwin residents, live in its sprawling northern suburbs. The expanding Bagot community, closer to the city centre, houses some three hundred, and the Kulaluk reserve at Coconut Grove provides a place for temporary residents.

There is no doubt that Darwin is expanding rapidly. The Territory has Australia's highest growth rate; in the year ended 30

Early morning clouds billow over oil storage tanks in Darwin

June 1984 it was 3.7 per cent, compared with a national figure of 1.15 per cent. The Territory also has a young population – in 1984 an estimated 71 per cent were under thirty-five, compared with a national figure of 57.3 per cent.

Despite these impressive growth figures the Territory's population is still quite small. At the end of June 1984 the estimate was 138,000 (somewhat larger than that of Townsville but a few thousand short of the population of Geelong), and just under half – 66,100 according to the 1984 estimate – live in Darwin.

Although Darwin reached city status in 1959, in comparison with other capitals it is still a big country town, but one whose politicians and entrepeneurs wish on it city sophistication and tourist magnetism. Many oldtimers long ago claimed that these things had already been achieved, and promptly shifted on down the track to Humpty Doo, Pine Creek or Katherine for a slower pace.

There are probably tens of thousands of people around Australia who have lived at least a year or so of their lives in Darwin, enjoyed it or not and moved on, holding good memories and bad. Some will even proudly claim it as their own experience of life on the fringe, survival in the harshest of conditions. But the conditions were a blessing during the 1930s depression, when many southern unemployed made their way north, in the hope of finding work, perhaps, but more likely to escape the cold of being homeless in a southern winter.

Darwin has always been known as a man's town, from its earliest days, when it was considered that white women were not suited to the climate. A few did come to Darwin – the wives and daughters of government men – and even fewer ventured to the Territory's isolated stations and hot dusty mining towns. The war brought another form of male dominion and Darwin retained the image for many years as a place for hard working, hard living and

Preparing a new oval, Sanderson High School

hard drinking. Today this is still its reputation, though the ratio of men to women is only slightly higher than the national ratio.

The isolation, together with the climate of the Top End, makes life here very different from the rest of Australia. Maximum temperatures rarely drop below 30°C in Darwin – in fact, the average daily temperatures in the coolest month, July, range from a minimum of 19 to a maximum of 30°C, while in the hottest month, November, the range is 25 to 33°C. Being able to work in air-conditioning is definitely an advantage, and the hum of air-conditioners and the whir of overhead fans are constant sounds of the suburbs. It's the sort of climate in which people are likely to declare the weather "a bit cool" if they have to sleep covered by a sheet.

Instead of four seasons, the Top End has basically two, the Wet and the Dry, with a transition period preceding the Wet known as the "build-up". If anything causes people to "go troppo" it is the oppressive heat and humidity of the build-up. From late October storm clouds loom but their promise of rain is often a hollow one and the days drag on. By January the Wet is usually entrenched but talk of late Wets and even dry Wets is common enough in some years to be less than humorous. The rain begins to ease off in April and by June there is virtually none at all until the cycle begins again. The average annual rainfall is 1652mm and the wettest Wet on record, with 2253mm, was that of 1974-75, the period in which Cyclone Tracy virtually wiped out Darwin.

In the early hours of Christmas Eve 1974 the cyclone rounded Bathurst Island, changing direction to head straight for Darwin. Most people were unprepared – cyclones always seemed to cause trouble elsewhere and Christmas festivities were the main preoccupation. Tracy's intensity was horrific. Wind gusts reached 217 kilometres per hour before the recording apparatus was wrecked. Few buildings escaped damage and most of Darwin's housing was

Sandblasting steel in the industrial suburb of Winnellie

destroyed. Worst hit were the northern suburbs; their development had been rapid and most of the new homes were flimsy. Much of the damage was caused by flying sheets of roofing iron and other debris. Trees were up-rooted, steel poles twisted, brick walls collapsed. The death toll was forty-nine in Darwin, another sixteen at sea.

Cyclone Tracy no doubt changed the face of Darwin both physically and in character. On Christmas Eve 1974 its population had numbered 46,000; by New Year's Eve 11,000 remained. They took on the job of cleaning up aided by the navy and then the army. It took only three and a half years for the population to reach its pre-cyclone level but, though many of its previous residents returned, the newcomers more easily imposed themselves on a city not simply being rebuilt but being built anew.

In pre-Tracy Darwin much of the population lived in government-built and government-furnished houses (curtains, floor coverings, furniture and colour schemes were all government issue) and the uniformity of the housing tended to remove any great class consciousness. Realizing now the importance of houses that were solid and sturdy, many of the new homes mimicked the architecture of the south, to the discomfort of their occupants. Government houses simply borrowed the designs for the sake of expediency without consideration for the climate. The place became more materially aware – for example, sarongs were soon no longer acceptable dress in the city streets.

Many businesses did not reopen and shops and buildings stood empty or were used only temporarily for a number of years before being pulled down, opening the way for development on a grander scale. The old Star Theatre, ever-popular but especially in the Dry for it was partially open-air, was badly damaged and the cinema was not revived.

Weather-beaten Studebaker, Lee Point

Darwin lost much of its early architecture. Though some of the stone buildings, such as the Victoria Hotel and Brown's Mart, were later reconstructed, many of the wide-verandahed and bamboo-shuttered tropical houses were totally destroyed. The few of these early timber houses that survived in the older suburbs are one by one being demolished in the name of progress, though some have been restored on-site or transported elsewhere. A new tropical architecture is beginning to creep back, however, using the elevated design and natural ventilation.

The inner-city area is going the way of most inner cities – up. Concrete and glass feature, but wide eaves and shaded windows are some consolation. Office blocks predominate but two new hotels are due to open in 1986, the Darwin Sheraton and the Beaufort Hotel attached to the Darwin Performing Arts Centre. Both are designed to attract the "international-class" tourist as well as the lucrative convention market.

But development is measured not only in terms of the construction of buildings and the expansion of suburbs. Darwin has been made a beautiful city; the wet season rains and the city council's extensive sprinkler systems ensure parks and gardens of lush tropical growth. Reserves such as East Point and Casuarina are popular and pleasant recreational areas.

Darwin is also surrounded by water – the somewhat murky harbour around the city centre and the Arafura Sea edging the suburbs. The beaches are attractive with their dramatically coloured cliffs fringed with casuarina trees. But for much of the year the water is dangerous. Lethal box jellyfish, erroneously known as sea-wasps, are flushed out of the mangrove swamps during the wet season so that from October to May the sea is off-limits. Dry season swimmers have trouble unless they take careful note of the tides. Darwin has a tidal range of a massive eight metres. Time it wrongly and you have to walk endlessly to catch more than knee-deep water.

Sheer sided walls of Katherine Gorge tower over the Katherine River

The image of hundreds of colourful sailing boats anchored off Vestey's Beach at Fannie Bay in the dry season, against bright blue water, is not easily forgotten. Sunsets are also one of Darwin's specialities and the beaches are the best vantage point as a giant sun dips into the sea.

The foreshore is also dotted with patches of mangrove swamp and tidal mudflats. The swamp areas are unsuited to residential development but provide a perfect environment for bird life and a breeding ground for marine life, including the estuarine crocodile. Many are removed from the harbour and tidal creeks around Darwin and taken to more suitable areas.

As Darwin grows, more people are moving into its rural area. Humpty Doo is best known for the abortive attempt there in the 1950s to grow rice. It was to be a large-scale project with American backing and the aim of exporting to Asia. Various management problems prevented it from becoming anything so grand and, when thousands of Magpie Geese demolished what crop there was, the project was abandoned. It left a legacy, however, in the form of Fogg Dam, now a wildlife refuge with abundant birdlife – including the Magpie Geese.

Howard Springs is another destination for day trippers from Darwin. Once a recreational area for the servicemen stationed in Darwin during the war, this nature park is popular more for its sedate swimming hole than abundant wildlife. The park, however, has managed to preserve a fragment of rainforest. Berry Springs Nature Park offers a similar setting, but with a greater area of rainforest. The clear warm water attracts people as its beautiful surrounding forest attracts birds – both are numerous.

About a hundred kilometres southwest of Berry Springs is a reserve tentatively known as the Tabletop Range Park. It is escarpment country, endowed with waterfalls, and the site of giant magnetic anthills up to four metres in height.

Sunset at Nightcliff Beach, Darwin

Anywhere outside Darwin is commonly known as "down the track" and there is no track longer than the Stuart Highway, from the heart of Darwin to Adelaide. South to Batchelor numerous airstrips stretch out beside the highway, relics of World War Two, and at Adelaide River the graves of the war dead are tended carefully. Batchelor itself was once the scene of the Territory's first copper mine, a coffee project and peanut farms.

Pine Creek is undergoing another gold boom, with open-cut mining expected to produce a half million gold ounces over a ten-year life span.

Further down the track to Katherine, and west to the Daly River area, the land has been utilised for cattle grazing and agricultural experimentation. It is littered with historic stations such as Springvale on the Katherine River, which started out in the 1870s with an attempt at grazing sheep; Elsey, of which Jeannie Gunn wrote the classic novel *We of the Never Never*, Newcastle Waters, Delamere, and the famous Victoria River Downs toward the western border.

But the pastoral industry was not the source of great wealth that first the South Australian government and then the Commonwealth had expected. Lack of a ready market and transport difficulties added to the more basic problem of an extremely harsh climate, of which there was no prior experience to guide the management of the stations.

Experimental farms thoughout the region suffered the same difficulties and many projects – with crops such as sugar cane, tobacco, coffee, maize, peanuts and sorghum – were attempted and abandoned during the past century. More recent efforts, however, are beginning to pay off, particularly on the experimental farms of the Douglas-Daly region. Sorghum, mung bean, soybean, peanuts and sesame seed are doing well and the Top End's horticultural

Samphire tidal mud flats, with rising tide, Gurig National Park,
Cobourg Peninsula

industry is one of its fastest growing. Agriculture and the beef industry are currently worth $80 million a year and employ more than 3,500 people.

Mining is still the Territory's wealthiest industry, with tourism a close runner-up. In the year to June 1984 mineral production was worth $786.9 million, half of it from uranium mining. Small operations recovering tin and tantalum from Bynoe Harbour and zinc, lead and silver from the Woodcutters site, both near Darwin, augment the larger mines – copper and gold at Tennant Creek, uranium in the Alligator Rivers region and bauxite at Nhulunbuy on the Gove Peninsula. Off the Gulf coast south of Nhulunbuy is Groote Eylandt, Aboriginal settlement and the site of a large and high-grade deposit of manganese which has been mined since 1965.

Other Aboriginal settlements include Elcho Island, home of the Galiwinku people; Bathurst and Melville islands north-west of Darwin, where the Tiwi have thriving communities; and the Cobourg Peninsula, also a nature reserve.

But it is Arnhem Land which dominates in the Top End, accounting for roughly half of its land. During the early settlement of the Territory, the people of this area fiercely resisted attempts by pastoralists to encroach on their land, forcing them to abandon their stations. Today its sheer size ensures that a part of the Aboriginal culture lives on, developing in its own way, free of any influence it does not invite. Indeed, standing at the border crossing on the East Alligator River in Kakadu, Arnhem Land looks most inviting, a true escape from the pressures of "civilised" life.

A monsoonal shower approaches Fogg Dam

Corner of Trower Road and
Dripstone Road

Amy Johnson Ave.

Corner of Mitchell Street
and Daly Street

Amy Johnson Ave.

Stuart Highway, Noonamah

Dick Ward Drive

Casuarina Drive

Carpentaria palms, Holmes Jungle, Darwin

Water lilies, Howard Springs

Low tide, Casuarina Beach

High tide, Casuarina Beach

Spring-fed creek flows through rainforest near the proposed
Tabletop Range Park

*Swollen by wet season rain, Katherine River surges through the
upper section of Katherine Gorge*

Pink lotus lily, Fogg Dam

Rainforest, Tolmer Falls, in the proposed Tabletop Range Park

Rainbow over pandanus, Ludmilla, Darwin

Salmon gum at sunrise, Pine Creek

Mangroves, Vanderlin Island, Gulf of Carpentaria

Gurig National Park on the southern side of Cobourg Peninsula

The moon sets behind magnetic anthills, Reynolds River Floodplain

*Gateway to the Top End. King River bridge on the Stuart Highway,
south of Katherine*

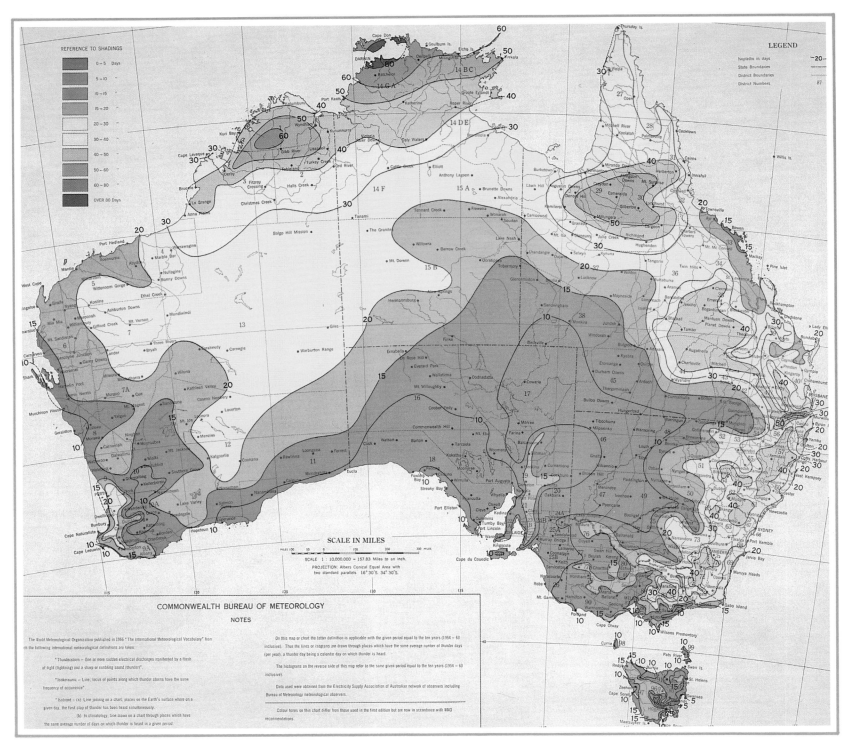

Average Annual Thunderday Map of Australia

Cloud Mountains of the Top End

3

The boys at the meteorological bureau have named him Hector. Old Hector is usually around from October to March. In the morning he's a ragged collection of scattered cloud. By midday the clouds have banded together and started to gain a fluffy appearance – the classic cotton-wool cloud. Driven by the heat of the sun, these innocuous clouds begin to push up, to the very limits of the earth's weather-producing atmosphere. Isolated pillars of cloud bulge upward, hesitate, then collapse downward again to produce a shower of rain. Then another column of cloud pushes, at enormous speed, to an even greater height this time, pauses to gather more energy and explodes in a burst of violent motion; it has literally run out of atmosphere. It has now reached the stratosphere and begins to flatten out at the top. Unable to pierce this barrier, the now mature thunderhead takes on its classic anvil-shaped top. Ominous rumbles of thunder permeate the sky and when the crack of a lightning bolt splits the rain drenched air, it is difficult not to accept Nature's dominance.

Hector is the thunderstorm which inhabits Melville Island. From September or October, his daily appearance is a feature of the view north from Darwin. His stance marks the position of Melville Island, where the thunderstorms develop out of the contrast between the heated land mass and the surrounding cooler sea. The island lies some eighty kilometres from Darwin's northern suburbs, but on a still day Hector's rumblings can be heard from Casuarina Beach. Occasionally, bolts of lightning leap from the anvil top of the thunderhead to the ground below, but in bright daylight and from such a distance the mind may doubt what the eye has seen. But when a second jagged line splits the air for a brief moment, there is no doubt; it was lightning.

Thunderstorms dominate the Top End sky for six months of the year. Awesome in their dimensions and grandeur, these wet season monoliths are the cloud mountains of the Top End. And mountains they are. Towering up to twenty kilometres

An enormous cloud front engulfs Nightcliff, Darwin, at low tide

above the predominantly flat land of the Top End, the pillars of cloud can be seen from 200 kilometres away, poking their capped heads into the stratosphere. An average thunderstorm may swell to some 7,000 cubic kilometres. These enormous dimensions are matched only by their staggering visual displays. Lightning of all types and colours stings the countryside, leaps from one cloud to another, and at night gently illuminates the cloud from within, showing intricate billowing patterns and delicate rain curtains.

The storms are steered by the unseen winds of the middle levels of the atmosphere, usually moving in a north-westerly direction through the Top End. Their grand passage through the hot, humid lowlands is announced by a menacing rumble and a rush of cooling wind giving people plenty of time to seek shelter from the impending tropical downpour.

In Darwin, this scenario occurs more often than in most other places in the world. The *Average Annual Thunderday Map of Australia* indicates that Darwin's ninety-odd thunderdays a year is the highest rate in Australia. Considering that they occur during seven months of the year only, the rate of thunderstorm activity can be considered quite remarkable – a thunderstorm would be in the vicinity of Darwin almost every other day for half the year.

But why so many thunderstorms? A combination of several factors working together, produces ideal conditions for their development. But these conditions occur as part of the overall weather pattern of Australia.

During the winter months, large high-pressure systems move across the Great Australian Bight from west to east, directing a consistent south-east wind across inland Australia. These south-easterlies are very dry and keep the weather over the Top End fine and dry for four or five months of the year.

A developing thunderstorm reflected in a flooded black soil plain,
Howard Springs

As the days become longer during August and September, the heat of the sun becomes more intense over northern Australia. The vast areas of rocky terrain in the Kimberlies of Western Australia and in Arnhem Land in the Top End absorb a massive amount of heat radiated from the incessant, scorching sun. This heating of the land causes a general uplifting of the air-mass over a large area, which in turn causes the barometric pressure to correspondingly fall. The result is what is termed a "heat low". By the end of October this heat low has become a semi-permanent feature of the weather map, and its presence forces the high-pressure cells of the Bight to move further south. This is when the weather of southern Australia begins warming up as the summer approaches.

Over the Top End, the previously south-east airstream swings around to the east and north-east, bringing with it tropical moisture and the chance of some early showers. As the heat low over the Kimberlies intensifies, the barometric pressure drops further and a system develops in which the low-pressure cell draws both an easterly and a northerly component of the airstream into this low. With two airstreams of differing origins being drawn into a single area, there is effectively more air flowing into a given area than that area can accommodate. So a squeezing effect is produced and the only place the air can go is up. This convergence is one of the main triggering mechanisms of the thunderstorms.

Meanwhile, this heating of the land mass continues right across northern Australia. The air becomes sufficiently heated to cause a trough to develop, emanating from the low over the Kimberlies, and extending for a distance of up to 1,000 kilometres to a similar heat low over inland Queensland. This trough, or dry-line, separates the moist tropical air of the north from the drier inland air of the south. The position of the trough fluctuates according to where the southern high-pressure cells are lying and, as this trough

An eerie reminder of the nuclear age, Casuarina, Darwin

moves from north to south through the Territory, it provides a further triggering mechanism for the thunderstorms.

The source for the formation of the heat low and heat trough is, of course, the sun. As it heats up the surface of the land, dynamic instability occurs – enough to cause large air-masses to be uplifted by convection currents. Add to this, orographic lifting over the Arnhem Land plateau, and you have a combination of conditions which are very conducive to thunderstorm development.

As the heat trough intensifies during December, the winds have a progressively more northerly component, until in early January, the north-west monsoon blows into the Top End, bringing with it buckets and buckets of rain. At this point, the heat trough joins with the monsoonal trough and the weather is then characterised by cloudy, showery days rather than the stark free-standing thunderstorms of the build-up period.

It is these components of the weather generating mechanisms which produce such dramatic clouds – the cloud mountains of the Top End.

Accompanying these enormous clouds are magnificent and dramatic displays of lightning. Frightening perhaps to a few, but awesome and intriguing to many, these night-time lightshows are a spectacle indeed. Several bolts every second may sometimes be seen, amounting to a stroboscopic effect. Unseen by the eye because of their rapidity, some bolts may flash and flicker up to fifty times, causing the lightning to linger for as long as two seconds. Other bolts may lazily run along the underside of middle-level cloud, left as residue from the passing torrent of rain. And the colour of the lightning can vary. Blue, yellow, purple and even green bolts have been seen. But the sheer number of lightning flashes is the most amazing of all. In December alone, Darwin can

A high-voltage discharge combines with a flaming sunset,
Nightcliff

record from 10,000 to 20,000 lightning flashes within an eighty kilometre radius – a staggering figure of 40,000 for the year! It is surely one of the most lightning-prone areas in the world; but surprisingly little damage to life or property occurs. A few lightning-struck trees are recorded each year and, certainly, any storm of reasonable intensity will cause failure of electricity supplies for a short while. During an intense storm, bolts of lightning have been known to strike electrical cables buried half a metre underground, and an ocean-going catamaran was sunk when a powerful bolt hit the boat's aluminium mast, then travelled down the mast and promptly punched a large hole in each hull. Fortunately no one was on board at the time.

For all its spectacular display and lethal power, lightning still remains much of a puzzle to science. It is known that the upper region of a thunderhead is positively charged while the base area is negatively charged. The cloud acts as an enormous electrostatic machine, building up electrical charges of opposing polarity to such a degree that air, which is normally an insulator, breaks down and forms a conductive channel. As much as 100 million volts may be generated in this way, discharging very large amounts of energy. Indeed, it has been estimated that lightning strikes about a hundred times per second around the world, representing an energy discharge of four billion kilowatts. It is also known that a positively charged "shadow" follows the thundercloud, induced by the strong negative charge. Hence, lightning discharges from the ground as well as from the upper regions of the cloud, to its base. But the actual mechanism for separating these charges is not understood.

Another little known fact is that when lightning discharges, the bolt actually moves from the ground up to the cloud and not, as is commonly believed, from the cloud to the ground. The lightning itself is visible electrical emission from charged cloud

*A purple lightning bolt delineates the rain area from the unusual
blue of a dawn sky, Casuarina*

and is only about five centimetres in diameter. The air around the discharge becomes superheated and white hot in colour, and so the lightning bolt appears much larger to the eye. As for thunder, it is the sound created by the rapid heating and expansion of gasses within the lightning channel.

Thunderstorms, for all their familiarity, still hold awe for most people. In temperate latitudes they bring days of rain and cold, but in the tropics their arrival is eagerly awaited. The strong downdraughts associated with the rain and the cloud cover generated, provide a welcome respite from the sun's scorching rays. But their occurrence is dramatically varied according to the month of the year. During September and October a few showers and the odd thunderstorm may occur but by December thunderstorms are in the vicinity of Darwin virtually every day. Although January and February are the wettest months of the year, this is attributable to the monsoon rather than thunderstorm activity. March sees another increase in thunderstorm frequency, but this tapers off quickly during April and May to once again establish the dry season weather pattern.

This seasonal wet-dry climate is a feature not only of Darwin but the whole of the Top End. The climate may be harsh but the spectacular wet season weather affords many hours of intriguing observation. Who could not be humbled by the incredibly intense rainfall, by the gigantic billowing clouds and by the ever-spectacular lightning displays? The dramatic clouds which roll through the Top End possess shape and form unrivalled by any. At the same time, the climate that creates them also shapes the environment and the people who inhabit this northern part of Australia.

Two bolts leap out of a decaying thunderstorm, Casuarina

A thunderstorm top creates a shadow line with the sunset, Fannie Bay, Darwin

An evening thunderstorm approaches Fannie Bay

A crescent moon tops a graduated sunset, Nightcliff

Early morning monsoonal shower over Francis Bay, Darwin

Sunrays burst from behind a billowing cloud, Nightcliff

With several layers of capping, enormous thunderheads push up at sunset, Humpty Doo

An unusual "half" sunset is effected by thunderstorms far over the horizon

A dark brooding cloud sits over Fannie Bay at sunset

A sunset thunderstorm is reflected in a wet season swamp,
Howard Springs

114

A large early morning thunderstorm directs lightning bolts over a large area, Casuarina

Early morning lightning over the sea, Casuarina

Lightning bolts punctuate the sky over Rapid Creek, Darwin

Dramatic single display of lightning, Howard Springs

ACKNOWLEDGEMENTS

Bureau of Meteorology, Melbourne, for use of the
Average Annual Thunderday Map of Australia.
Paul Nockolds for the preparation of the maps of
The Top End and *Kakadu National Park.*

SOURCES

Australian National Parks and Wildlife Service, *Kakadu National Park Plan of Management*
Ian Butterworth, Bureau of Meteorology, Darwin
Anne Ring, Bureau of Meteorology, Melbourne
Australian Bureau of Statistics, Darwin
P.P. Courtenay, *Northern Australia.* Melbourne: Longman Cheshire, 1982
Peter Forrest, *Springvale's Story.* Darwin: Murranji Press, 1985
Conservation Commission of the Northern Territory
Northern Territory Tourist Commission
Suzanne Parry, *That's Our Territory!* Brisbane: The Jacaranda Press and Northern Territory Department of Education, 1984
Alan Powell, *Far Country,* Carlton: Melbourne University Press, 1982
Protocol and Public Relations Unit, Department of the Chief Minister, Northern Territory
School of Australian Linguistics
Charles See-Kee, N.T. Ethnic Communities Council